Pebble
Plus

Life around the World
Transportation in Many Cultures

by Martha E. H. Rustad

Consulting Editor: Gail Saunders-Smith, PhD

Capstone
press®

Mankato, Minnesota

Pebble Plus is published by Capstone Press,
151 Good Counsel Drive, P.O. Box 669, Mankato, Minnesota 56002.
www.capstonepress.com

Library of Congress Cataloging-in-Publication Data
Rustad, Martha E. H. (Martha Elizabeth Hillman), 1975–
    Transportation in many cultures/by Martha E. H. Rustad.
    p. cm. — (Pebble plus. Life around the world)
    Summary: "Simple text and photographs present transportation in many cultures" — Provided
    by publisher.
    Includes bibliographical references and index.
    ISBN-13: 978-1-4296-1744-4 (hardcover)
    ISBN-10: 1-4296-1744-6 (hardcover)
    ISBN-13: 978-1-4296-3379-6 (softcover)
    ISBN-10: 1-4296-3379-4 (softcover)
    1. Transportation — Juvenile literature. I. Title. II. Series.
HE152.R87 2009
388 — dc22
                                         2008004188

Editorial Credits
Sarah L. Schuette, editor; Kim Brown, book designer; Alison Thiele, set designer; Wanda Winch, photo researcher

Photo Credits
Art Life Images/age fotostock/Sylvain Grandadam, 21
Capstone Press/Karon Dubke, 9
The Image Works, Lee Snider, 7; SV-Bilderdienst/Margrit Jordan, 13; Visum/Frank Aussieker, 11
Landov LLC/DPA/Roland Scheidemann, 5
Peter Arnold/Paul van Riel, cover; R. Hicker, 19
Shutterstock/gary718, 1; Ivan Cholakov, 17; Thorsten Rust, 15

Note to Parents and Teachers

The Life around the World set supports national social studies standards related to
culture and geography. This book describes and illustrates transportation in many
cultures. The images support early readers in understanding the text. The repetition of
words and phrases helps early readers learn new words. This book also introduces early
readers to subject-specific vocabulary words, which are defined in the Glossary section.
Early readers may need assistance to read some words and to use the Table of Contents,
Glossary, Read More, Internet Sites, and Index sections of the book.

Table of Contents

Transportation

People travel

in every culture.

Let's see how other people

around the world travel.

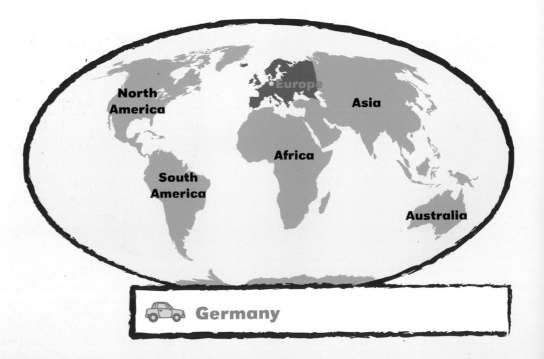

North America

Europe

Asia

Africa

South America

Australia

Germany

Going to School

These girls in China
walk to school.

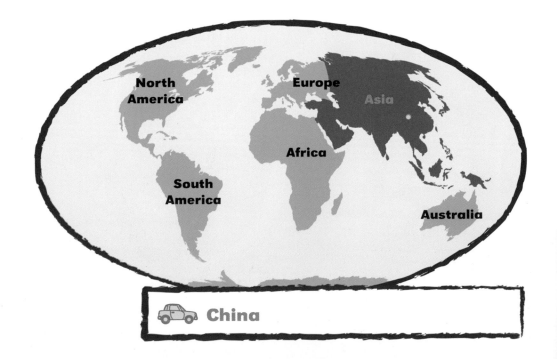

North
America

Europe

Asia

Africa

South
America

Australia

China

These boys in
the United States
ride a bus to school.

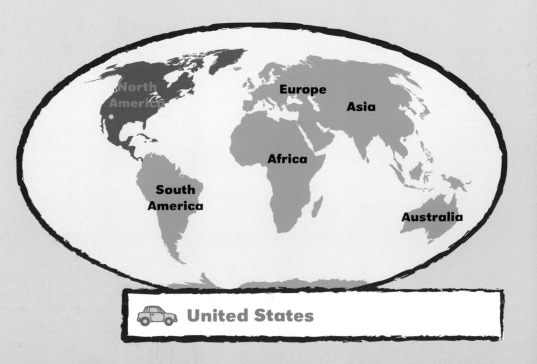

North
America

Europe

Asia

Africa

South
America

Australia

United States

These girls in Japan

ride a train to school.

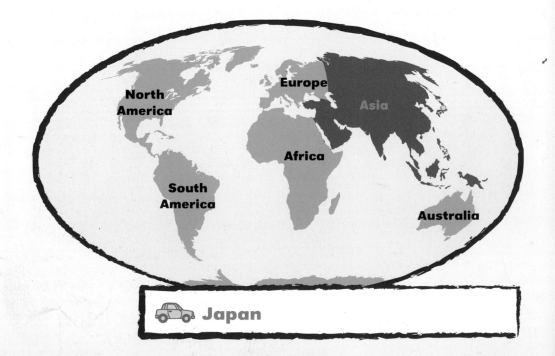

North America

Europe

Asia

Africa

South America

Australia

Japan

These kids in Cambodia
paddle boats to get
to their floating school.

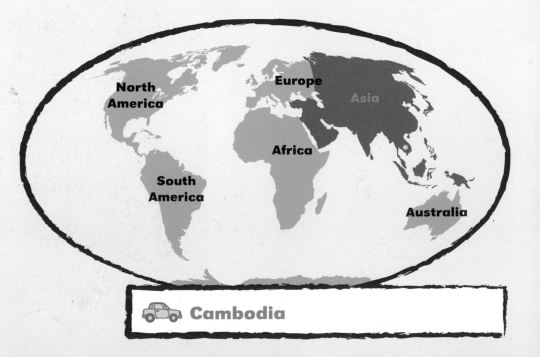

North
America

Europe

Asia

Africa

South
America

Australia

Cambodia

Going Other Places

People in Australia

ride the monorail.

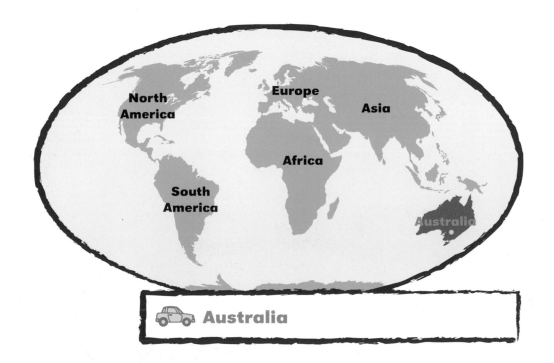

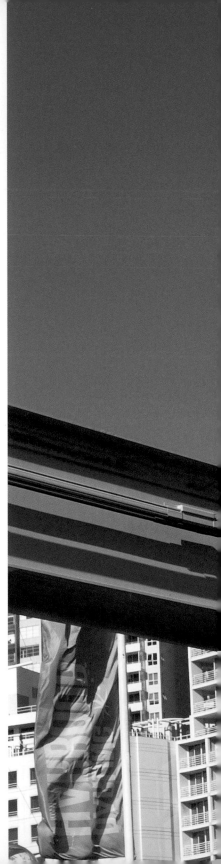

Australia

Travelers in Bolivia
take an airplane
to another country.

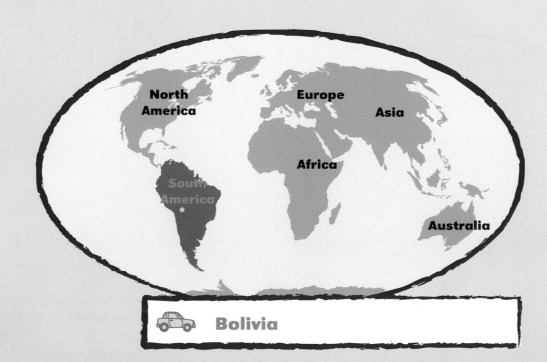

A boy in Canada

rides a snowmobile.

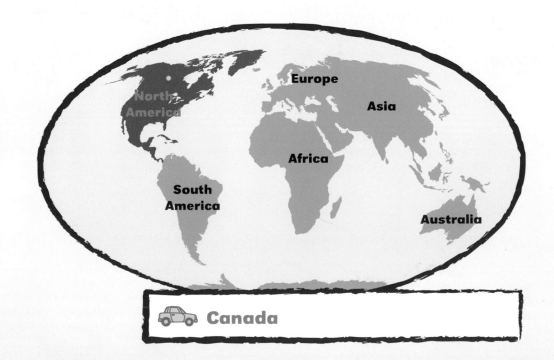

North America

Europe

Asia

Africa

South America

Australia

Canada

On the Go!

Around the world,

people ride buses, bicycles,

and animals.

How will you travel today?

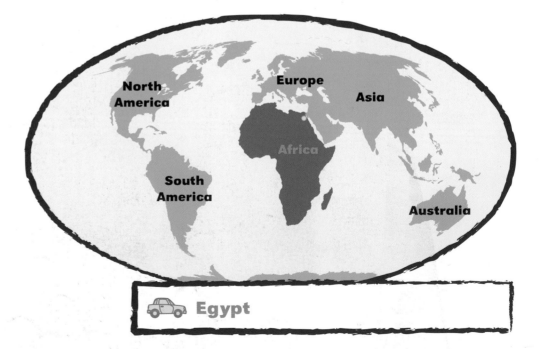

Egypt

Glossary

culture — the way of life, ideas, customs, and traditions of a group of people

monorail — a train that runs on one rail, usually high off the ground

paddle — to push through the water with an oar

snowmobile — a vehicle with skis used to travel over snow

travel — to go from one place to another

Read More

Guin, Valerie. *On the Move.* One World. North Mankato, Minn.: Smart Apple Media, 2006.

Mattern, Joanne. *Transportation.* Yesterday and Today. San Diego: Blackbirch Press, 2004.

Weber, Rebecca. *How We Travel.* Spyglass Books. Minneapolis: Compass Point Books, 2004.

Internet Sites

FactHound offers a safe, fun way to find Internet sites related to this book. All of the sites on FactHound have been researched by our staff.

Here's how:

1. Visit *www.facthound.com*

2. Choose your grade level.

3. Type in this book ID **1429617446** for age-appropriate sites. You may also browse subjects by clicking on letters, or by clicking on pictures and words.

4. Click on the **Fetch It** button.

FactHound will fetch the best sites for you!

Index

Word Count: 89
Grade: 1
Early-Intervention Level: 18